# You Can Make Anything Sad

Spencer Madsen

sorry house

Published by Sorry House

First edition April 2014 from Publishing Genius

Second edition February 2015



ISBN: 978-0-9888394-2-7

Cover design by Erik Carter

Page design by Adam Robinson

For distribution or wholesale information,
visit sorry.house

More like a stopped clock is always right.

–Blake Butler

# You Can Make Anything Sad

## Wednesday, September 26th, 2012

Watch as I impose on you new forms of useless emotions you didn't know existed.

Watch as everything becomes something worth regretting.

Smelling clean like a shower. Apologizing to my mother.

Today is a new day, like every other.

I have an urge to spend $250,000 to market a new book online.

Everyone gets the same empty envelope.

Mailing books has taught me that some addresses are short and nice and some are long and humiliating.

The key to not being an asshole is to realize when someone else is being vulnerable.

Whenever I have an uncomfortable interaction with someone I want to say, "Look I'm a lot like you. We have a lot in common. We're both going to die."

Then poke them in the stomach to make them giggle.

## Thursday, September 27, 2012

A state of the union address regarding my face:

"Things can only get worse."

People go to such lengths to believe there's more to life after death.

They would have much more time if they would just accept it. Nothing is good.

Mostly what I want is to wake up and not do the bad things that I am presented with each day.

Raise your hand if I'm attracted to you.

It's morning for one more minute.

I'm afraid if I begin to say goodbye it will cut me off and become noon.

Sitting here in underwear and socks, what can I do.

Neither fashion nor function.

A one person uniform.

## Friday, September 28, 2012

I was at a sports bar last night.

I went up to an attractive girl and said, "Hi."

She said, "Hello" with a thick accent and I suddenly realized she was French.

I said, "Michel Gondry."

She said, "Yes."

I said, "Movies."

## Saturday, September 29, 2012

Pickup line: Are you me.

Heritage is important.

I am eating the Trader Joes Teriyaki Meat Substitute of my ancestors.

It looks like cat food, as is tradition.

I got off work early today.

There were no customers.

The bosses came by and saw us all standing around.

They said, "Who wants to go home!"

I said, "Spencer."

Then I got to leave.

Which is good, because I was prepared to yell "FLOM FLOM FLOM FLOM FLOM," at anyone who might walk in.

I know that someone–many people, probably–died today, but I can't be certain because I didn't see anyone die.

It's a type of religion, this belief, that even when you aren't suffering, someone else is.

I texted Keila about it.

She agreed. I asked what she was up to.

She told me that octopi and squid both belong to the cephalopoda family.

Which, translated from Greek, literally means "head-feet."

## Sunday, September 30, 2012

Today was a day. It still is.

It never isn't.

It's either one day or another but it's never something in between.

It doesn't take much to ruin a day for me.

Treat me poorly for just a second.

Dare you.

Double dare you.

Double doggy dare you to make me feel bad.

The thing is, I'm not very good.

Some people walk down the sidewalk and they seem very good and they are usually walking past me, in the opposite direction, and maybe that's why.

A new dance gaining popularity across the country is called *seeming better than me momentarily as we pass each other on the sidewalk.* It's sweeping the nation, making me feel bad everywhere I go.

Today at work Jon said "Writing up work-orders is my job," emphasizing "my job" and maintaining eye contact with me.

It was the look of someone who has regrets, and their life has come to this, right now.

You can imagine the stakes.

Or maybe you can't.

Maybe you're good.

Maybe you're walking past me, out of my view and into a cluster of useless ideas that slow me down all the time, especially when I'm about to open my mouth or urinate in a public restroom.

I immediately forgave Jon.

He is not good.

He is like me.

He cuts his own hair.

He lives in my neighborhood.

We have similar jobs.

His job involves writing work orders. Mine apparently doesn't.

The difference between us is a few years and a few more reasons to give up, each one decreasing the likelihood of change, decreasing the likelihood of improving it or ending it, each one making it all more bearable, expected, comforting.

Continuing to live for logical reasons.

No need to rush.

Just be patient and you'll die eventually.

## Monday, October 1, 2012

When you turn the screen brightness down on your computer, everything looks the same but seems a little shittier.

That's what it's like to be me.

What did I do today.

I bought a gym membership and made Keila feel bad.

The guy who signed me up at the gym was strong and had spiked hair.

He had three tattoos: ♫ ☠ ☢

I kept thinking "The real thing, he's the real thing."

His tattoos are meaningless, his hairstyle too, even his muscles (he does administrative work). In a way though, he is more authentic than I am. His body is more purely veneer. A more empty facade. Music. Pirates. Radiation.

His tattoos were probably chosen out of a tattoo book.

The kind of pre-fab creativity that brings us closer to not choosing at all. A day that would turn from morning to noon without anyone running late. The illusion we have of controlling time would fade like lost children. Dead in a shallow grave or eating cake out of a dumpster behind 7/11.

There's so much hope imbued in those gone missing.

I am always exactly where I am.

## A NEW REALITY SHOW CALLED:

A new reality show called *Is this it* where people do things for the first time and think is this it.

A new reality show called *I'm single* in which a person sleeps with a body pillow, buys eggs in half-dozen containers, and doesn't bother brushing their teeth before bed.

A new reality show called *Did I lock my front door* in which people look vaguely confused for a few seconds before remembering whether or not they locked their front door.

A new reality show called *Is it okay to eat this* in which people read the expiration dates of various foods in their fridge and smell them suspiciously.

A new reality show called *I wish I didn't have to pee* that consists of people lying down comfortably in bed and then suddenly having to pee.

A new reality show called *All I want to do is sit down* in which people work jobs that require standing for a long periods of time for low wages.

## Tuesday, October 2, 2012

Just cleaned my room.

Feels good.

Why don't I do the things that feel good.

My stomach hurts and so does knowing.

I used a chemical spray to wipe down my desk.

My head and tummy are spinning in opposite directions.

I wonder if this is what it's like to be pregnant.

It's probably nothing like this, right.

This is more like eating some slightly-expired seafood.

What if that's how you got pregnant?

I feel really dumb today and it doesn't feel like my fault.

I sit at this desk in front of a window

There's a dog that barks outside every day for hours.

I imagine every time his owner goes to work and he's left by himself, he thinks "This is it, she's really going this time. She's really gone."

Then the barking starts. Not because he's angry, but because he's scared. He doesn't want to be alone.

So I don't mind the barks much.

I've been there.

## Thursday, October 4, 2012

Sitting in a cafe now.

Finally getting to work.

I need to be in the place for the thing to do the thing.

I won't exercise unless I'm in a gym.

I won't study unless I'm in a library.

I won't get any writing done unless I'm in a cafe.

I'm setup at a table that edges into the aisle.

I'm in the way, but I like it. I get to apologize to people. They apologize back. It's reciprocal.

The best response to "I'm sorry" will always be "I'm sorry."

The best response to "I hate myself" will always be "I hate myself."

The best response to "I love you" will always be "I love you."

The best response to "I'm scared" will always be "I am too."

The only dirty talk I want to hear during sex is apologetic.

## Sunday, October 7, 2012

It's the first cold day of the end of the year.

The sky is lit like a cold gymnasium.

Nothing has changed size.

If you look at it, as a whole, like a clock turning and adding more seconds on, it's all internal, the mechanisms. It doesn't affect the size of the object, no matter how much it moves forward.

But the seasons are changing.

I say hello and they keep moving.

It's all the same in terms of size.

I want to say goodbye to people I haven't met and to know what it feels like to pass by everything always—to have been present this whole time until now.

Time is the never-ending but always-ending goodbye. Progressing toward no end other than a polished black surface, breathing forgiveness as it has what it wants.

It doesn't feel good.

## Monday, October 8, 2012

I want you to make it a challenge for me to love you.

The things that are hardest to love are the things we love most.

If I had a "type" it would probably be grieving girls.

I'm sorry.

I wish elves were at least sort of real, like dwarves.

Last night I shut my windows to seal the warmth of my body inside my bed.

Soon after waking I put on long wool socks and made coffee.

Outside it's cloudy and not very beautiful, but when I look out at the sky my face feels younger.

I look at it like I am its child, unsure of everything but trusting of something.

I read poems by my friends.

I feel something for the poems and something for my friends.

In the age of the internet, people very far away can hurt you.

When it's done beautifully, in the way of a poem, the pain is calming.

Tomorrow is Tuesday and I think if I didn't have to be alive, Tuesday would be my favorite day.

It's getting cold before it's getting orange and it's getting gray before getting yellow.

Winter is overtaking fall. It's the season of succumbing to the cold but it's giving in too soon.

The houses usually decorated with pumpkins and people are silent and defensive.

It's hard to imagine anything but Tuesdays everyday.

## IDEAS:

A form of therapy called *It doesn't get better.*

Bipartisan political party called *We are all going to die.*

A tumblr called *Girls doing things* featuring photos of fully clothed girls doing normal things like standing in line at the post office or walking a dog.

An internship called *Scared and needy.*

A brand of whiskey called *This won't make you a better writer.*

A brand of cosmetics called *Afraid of dying.*

A t-shirt that says *I'm not this.*

Instead of asking your neighbors "How are you?" try "Yes or no."

A dictionary that translates *avant-garde*, loosely, as *asshole.*

A body pillow shaped computer case.

A dentist's office called *First world problems.*

A religion called *More scared than everyone else.*

A porno where two people begrudgingly apologize to each other and sit in silence because the apologies seemed forced and there's clearly more talking to do.

## Tuesday, October 9, 2012

I have this very uncomfortable feeling of doing nothing. Just sitting. Trying to get rid of it. Eating excessively. Masturbating excessively.

Too occupied with myself to leave my apartment, or read a book, or watch a movie.

I need to have rough sex or get into a fight.

But neither of those things are possible, given my isolation and nature.

It's like restless leg syndrome, only my whole life.

I want to do something insane but I want the insane thing to be presented to me when I walk into the living room.

I have gotten nothing done and I realize that the true reason I need to go to a cafe to write is because I can't masturbate in a cafe.

## Wednesday, October 10, 2012

It's 12:30pm but it feels like morning.

Listening to songs ruined by voices.

Drinking coffee. Eating toast.

Hell yeah.

I'm the Sasha Grey of eating this toast.

This is life.

This is real life.

This is my real life.

I'm experiencing an entirely similar phenomenon to millions of other people. I understand why no one is freaking out.

I'm tired and they might be too.

The sun, though pleasant and comforting on my skin, lays itself slowly and heavily into my muscles.

It's like blankets and pillows, it makes nothing, or rather the space between things, seem like the best thing.

I look at my last piece of toast and think "Goodbye. I love you, you little fucker."

I look at my hands typing and I make fun of them, only without words, because that's how my brain interacts with my body.

There are no words inside me. There are only sounds and thoughts. Words come later, like any disappointment.

I'm always trying to be a better person.

What if I put a sign outside my door, for all my roommates to see, that said: THE MASTURBATORIUM.

Would that be more honest.

I'm trying to figure it all out.

I used to think I did.

After a long relationship once, I spent a longer time alone.

I looked at myself after stunted months, sitting or sleeping.

I saw that I was okay.

I was sitting in this same chair thinking: I'm okay.

It wasn't until later that I realized I was just filling the quiet of my thoughts with words from podcasts and records and the street outside while I ran at night, people having sex on my computer screen and the internal crashing of mastication.

When the immediacy of mortality and the urgency of being alone manifests itself inside me, that's when I'm at my best. That's when I read, write, and run the most. That's when I'm the least content with where I am, why I'm here, and what I'm doing with that knowledge.

Understanding how to proceed is all of it.

Understanding that people are always a worse version of who they want to be is a way of loving them.

Understanding that saying goodnight can be the kindest thing you can do, if done right, eyes hard and soft.

## Thursday, October 11, 2012

Yesterday the king of Sealand died.

I am still mourning.

Sealand is two cylinders in the water off the coast of England that support a platform on which sits a house and a helipad.

It was used as a military facility in World War II.

Then it was taken over by pirate-radio broadcasters.

Then the Late King of Sealand took it from the pirate-radio broadcasters to broadcast his own pirate-radio.

Then he was like, Wait no. I am king. This is my nation.

Now he's dead.

Sealand's first king is gone.

I walked around outside and no one seemed to care.

A barely audible ring is heard as you watch yourself
in the mirror, trying to see yourself age in real time,
your phone cheering you on.

## Friday, October 12, 2012

I wonder about the extremely beautiful people.

The people who you can't imagine sleeping with, even in the back room of your mind where that sort of thought dies over and over again. The people who your brain immediately blurs into periphery as you pass them by.

As they pass you by.

The people who exist simultaneously in two dimensions, seeming to walk and breathe in the same reality as everyone else, but with the impression they're just visiting for some obligatory reason, a tiresome dinner reservation, a meeting over drinks.

I wonder, do they ever dribble a little when they drink beverages.

I dribble sometimes.

Or else I burst into a fit of coughs because I swallowed the wrong way.

I wonder, do they ever pop their pimples.

If they ever get pimples, I mean.

I heard from several people over the years that it's not good to pop your pimples. Just leave them alone, they would tell me.

Is that the mistake I made?

Is that where the line was drawn? Where the extremely beautiful people made their departure from the rest of us?

Because I love popping pimples.

I wouldn't give it up for anything.

## Saturday, October 13, 2012

The most basic subtext of everything cats do is "Fuck you love me."

The most basic subtext of everything people put on the internet is "Hello."

Trying to eat all the avocados in my apartment before they go bad is a good exercise in mortality.

Seeing an attractive couple make out in public is the same thing as knowing you're going to die.

Being a teenager means having enough hope to think you're alone in feeling miserable.

Children should be taught from a young age, "No one cares about you as much as you care about you."

The place you matter most is inside your room.

## Sunday, October 14, 2012

Lying in bed with Keila.

I put her on top of me and think, God damn it, I'm going to write poems about you.

It's a feeling like knowing you'll have to go to church on Sunday.

Her hair was draped around me and I was inside its circle.

I looked up at her.

She was pretty.

Maybe you can quantify these things.

Words about other things.

Words that connect with each other like puzzle pieces from different puzzles.

You can push them all together.

## Monday, October 15, 2012

Cereal and milk is a poor substitute for ice cream, which is a poor substitute for emotional stability.

I took a long shower today.

Sometimes when I take long showers I have the same recurring thought the whole time.

It's usually nonsense, like "Do what the wop does to you. Do it wop. Do it you. Wop one. Wop two."

I'm sitting at my desk now and looking out the window.

I see a bird that looks like the Twitter bird and ask it how to get more followers.

There are times where I walk around outside wearing headphones, seeing how almost everything people do is an attempt to get other people to touch them.

Time is an algorithm for more pain than you had before.

Dandruff is evidence that you are constantly falling apart in small, barely perceptible, unappealing ways.

Waiting for the future is the only thing you can do your whole life.

## Tuesday, October 16, 2012

The illusion of relationships is the lessening of distance but a new distance arises when a stranger becomes a friend.

Now suddenly palpable is how little can be shared between two individuals.

Out of this insecurity grows expectations.

Unspoken guidelines to ensure comfort down the line.

Strangers, however, expect nothing of each other because the distance between them is so great.

It follows that a small gesture can mean so much.

The smile after a fumble of papers that says, hey, things don't always go well.

That's the face we should keep ready for each other all the time.

No matter how far away everyone is.

# WOULD READ A SELF-HELP BOOK CALLED:

Would read a self-help book called *How to know when to quit: Life Edition.*

Would read a self-help book called *How to feel productive on the internet.*

Would read a self-help book called *How to react when someone grinds on you.*

Would read a self-help book called *How to think of carrying a backpack as anything other than giving it a piggyback ride.*

Would read a self-help book called *How to stop feeling like you're still trying to make up for something you did wrong at age six.*

Would read a self-help book called *How to come to terms with the part of yourself that looks for hyper-personal life-altering epiphanies inside self-help books.*

## Friday, October 19, 2012

There are some colors that only certain butterflies and seafloor creatures can perceive.

We only see a portion of the color spectrum.

And emotions are a similar thing. We can only occupy a small portion of the spectrum at any given time, while another person might occupy a totally different portion altogether.

I understand relationships in the way that nutritional facts tell you what's inside of something without demonstrating what it looks like or how it tastes.

I read nutritional facts and meaning falls away as instructions take their place.

A new emotion I'm feeling is called Everyday.

It's also a scent, color, taste, and texture.

The closest reference point is any monument to anything anywhere, shaped for a reason that will be forgotten, smoothed by hands and then by time, nicer to touch when no one is left to touch it.

Look at me when I am talking to you from distances you cannot see and at volumes you cannot hear.

I am always north.

Hide me in your backpack.

As I was crossing the street last night a car slowed down next to me. The driver rolled down his window and asked “Where the strip joints at?” I said, “I don’t know” and he said “Man, what’s wrong.”

## Monday, October 22, 2012

Today doesn't seem like a new day.

It's 3:32 pm.

I sit here with:

An empty mug

A dirty plate

A chapstick, dry without a cap.

A pen from a bank I don't belong to.

These are the things on my desk that I am currently moving with through time.

And also everything everywhere.

All things are coming with me forward into the future or backwards into the past.

A new new new new new something.

Never ever always once a person does a do and dies.

Raise me up with your eyebrows. Train for this by questioning everything.

A new new.

The post-new of yesterday and always tomorrow.

I'm stuck in a loop of thoughtless interface, my brain on both pause and repeat.

I almost ended everything with Keila and instead pushed farther into something deeper and darker with less visible light through the cluster of arms on top of moving arms between below and above more arms reaching for time and reaching for each other.

How much of everything can I buy with money I don't have and from people I don't know in places I've never been.

My desk is more a place for my hair to fall and nails to yellow than for my brain to think or hands to move. If you look close enough at the wood-grain lacquer you will find curly thin hairs that were once a part of me. Dying calmly in fractions of a billion, my desk holy.

A new-new.

Grasping for something in another person, the way seats on the train become available right before your stop.

The anxiety of relationships, not knowing whether everything matters or nothing matters.

The presence of things like embarrassment.

The way a mirror exists through the sense it doesn't make, conveying in front of you what's behind you.

And yeah.

There isn't anything more comforting than switching my chat status to invisible.

And in terms of everything, it is completely possible to compare apples to oranges. They have different colors and similar makeup, the orange is round, like certain apples, though closer to a sphere. The apple varies in color more with the type and the season. The orange has a thicker skin that's easier to peel. Both grow from trees, both have a stem. The stem, which accounts for their existence, always gets in the way.

And if nothing is truly disparate, than there is some sort of interconnectivity to all matter, something not just material like carbon or hydrogen, but written within our most basic perception, where we are able to see that blue and yellow sort of convey the same thing even though they are different colors, that a rough surface can be used to make things soft.

And I knew at a young age, stepping out of the school bus as the red stop sign opened from the side, that we need protection from the oncoming.

And from this young age I began to understand things like time, the way a song can mean something in spite of its lyrics.

And I felt interested in growing up and creating something enormous, something demanding of attention that would occupy mountains like eras.

That changed in me. This age, I want worldwide indifference when I wake up late for work.

The creation of absence is what I want to achieve most.

A stark nothingness, striking in everything it isn't.

And I wait for tomorrow and think of some girl who isn't really making eye contact with me, just thinking inwards while I exist as scenery for her commissionless eyes till she comes back to her immediate surroundings and sees me looking at her and she looks away.

I'm always waiting.

Buildings close in around me, this city.

Pulled against a body I can't ever push through.

Party people enter in pairs, complete happy couples, as if they just come that way.

It’s 4:14.

The things with which I move through time have stopped moving.

## A NEW DANCE CALLED:

A new dance called *please don't look at me.*

A new dance called *some babies look like weird fish.*

A new dance called *emotionally abusive relationship status on Facebook.*

A new dance called *are they any flights that go to my childhood.*

A new dance called *disappointed by this coffee and other decisions I've made in my recent history.*

A new dance called *talking to your parents becomes increasingly depressing and necessary as you get older.*

A new dance called *crying in public places for no discernible reason.*

A new dance called *things you don't want to do but should do but don't have to do but you do anyway.*

A new dance called *wishing I was someone else but that person didn't have to be me.*

## Tuesday, October 23, 2012

It always seems hostile to me, in music videos, when girls shake their asses really vigorously.

Like they are doing battle.

I'm seated in the back this time at the Crosby.

The trees are out, fighting the good fight.

The barista commented on their color.

But maybe trees aren't so beautiful in themselves.

Maybe they are beautiful because they obstruct our view of whatever's behind them.

They are beautiful because for slivers of space we don't have to see other people, or look at them and feel seen.

Comforted by their indifference despite their presence.

The music is some kind of funk, made to sound both new and old, striving to transcend the lifespan of culture.

With my laptop I sit here, a premium assface.

If writing really were masturbation I'd be so much better at it.

I tab around different sites, many redundant, looking at Twitter then opening it again in a new tab.

I log on to okcupid, a social network for girls who make me anxious.

The key to okcupid, I've found, is to make your profile into a depressingly neurotic and incoherent mess so that no one messages you or responds to your messages.

I move back to Facebook, I type:

If you feel an aversion to me and I don't feel an aversion to you, please don't feel an aversion to me.

I think about how my parents had hoped for more.

I think about letting them down constantly.

I think, at least I'm not a murderer.

Mostly because murderers are very ambitious.

## Wednesday, October 24, 2012

Another gathering of the plaid last night.

It sometimes takes an old internet security question in the morning, like your favorite color, to remind you of how inconsistent you are with your past selves.

Making introductions, my body a trailer playing during the movie it's advertising. Muffling it's nice to meet you.

The easiest thing to impose on other people is your own insecurities.

It's a kind of narcissism, this belief, that anyone would care about your stupid face.

There should be a certain physical stance for when you talk to yourself under the guise of having a conversation with someone else, so that, considerately, you can both disengage into it.

Locked up my bike and waited drunk for the train.

For once, when I sneeze on a subway platform, I would like to hear a bless-you from across the tracks, from someone waiting on the other side.

I want to traverse that distance, of futures headed in opposite directions, with a thank you.

And it's in the darkest of moments that I worry the closest we can get to telepathy is winning a game of rock paper scissors.

## Sunday, October 28, 2012

A hurricane is coming. Hurricane Sandy.

Keila says she isn't scared because all the Sandys she knows are dogs and dogs are usually good.

The sky is fucked in a way that softens my room.

I feel tired and my head feels heavy. I thank this pillow for putting up with me, though I feel like an asshole because I know it doesn't have a choice, so now I feel sorry.

Some days I can convince myself that socializing is just going to a thing, and if the people are shitty then I'll just leave, and the whole time I'll just be the person I'm inside of, a relief of guilt because what can you do.

And some days that doesn't work, like telling someone in a fit of rage to calm down, the words sounds.

And if those are two types of days, then this is a third, where I'm not convinced or unconvinced, nor am I in between. I just have no opinion, not winning or losing because I'm not playing. The world turns at exactly the rate things take shape and colors spread out. I look at this screen as it dries my eyes and I feel the possibility of a slow death this way, and it seems fine, like calling in late to work, using a sick day, talking about going out of town but not really going anywhere, buying an instrument to put in storage, listening to the same songs and watching the same television shows and the only things that ever change are the commercials in between.

The saddest Disney song will always be Peter Pan's I Won't Grow Up.

## Monday, October 29, 2012

The trees are waving. Sideways crashes of serrated water.

The hurricane has killed 22 people so far.

There's a kid in a baseball cap and a rain jacket riding his scooter around outside my building.

He gives no fucks.

I ate pasta earlier and now I feel the olive oil pushing its way through my face.

Keila says her favorite pasta is orecchiette because they look like tiny hats.

I'm listening to specific music in an attempt to feel a certain way. I'm writing to specify what I'm feeling.

School has taught me to believe I should be specific.

My 7th grade teacher, Mr. Lyons, used to reprimand my class for using the word *stuff*. We were supposed to say exactly what we meant.

But that assumes we meant anything.

Last night my coworker came by the shop drunk and red-faced after we closed up. It was his day off. His eyes were bigger than usual. I asked if he was looking for a fight. He said he's looking to feel.

Now I feel a certain affection towards him.

Listening to this music is like sitting in the same waiting room you go to when getting better becomes both the only option and the most impossible one.

The place where you can't wait for the wait to be over.

This past summer I ate fried chicken and wondered why anyone even bothers to write in a world where there's fried chicken.

I want to remember that feeling. I want to begin thinking that thought from the beginning again.

I remember being in a room with a bed identical to all the other efficient rooms down the hall.

I remember the weather. Wearing a t-shirt felt like mischief.

I remember walking across to my girlfriend's room. Knowing something's wrong. Feeling like I'll never get accustomed to the constant knowledge that something's wrong.

Every morning felt like a job interview.

Every night tired and scared, but not enough of either.

I remember running late at night. I remember the 24-hour gym. I remember running in place for hours on machines that ensure no actual progress. I remember sweating in the industrial blue glow.

I remember the feeling of winter coming.

## Tuesday, October 30, 2012

The subways are flooded.

The lines that go under the East River and connect Brooklyn to Manhattan are filled with water.

This feels right, waterlogged subways. Rapid conversations, eyes soaking into heads, driftwood magazines, advertisements screaming for hands.

And every train that came before a train you missed.

Soon my laundry will be dry, and then I will go get it, and then I will fold it, and hang it, and stare at it, and move on.

I wonder about the Australians and New Zealanders. I wonder if their perception of American poetry is different because their seasons are switched, the names of months retaining different associations, December's warmth, July's cold.

And I wonder if it matters.

But I don't wonder about that long.

Maybe a second and a half.

That's as much as I can spare, right now.

Hurricane. You know.

And yeah. It's sort of selfish to apologize for something you did wrong, because under the guise of humbling yourself you are actually telling the person to comfort you for your error, and tell you it's okay.

I tried to tell Keila this.

*I realize, in editing, how selfish I can be.*

## Saturday, Nov 3, 2012

I'm attracted to people who look like how I want to feel.

It's daylight savings time tomorrow.

It all comes an hour harder.

Trying to write a tweet is like trying to get someone to like you.

The longest tweet ever recorded is 140 characters. In the future, all world records will be equally unimpressive.

Not enough people see through me, some people talk to me like I'm fine.

I want to hunt rabbits with toy rifles. I'll say "bang" after aiming at them from a distance. I will hug them dearly and then let them go.

## Sunday, Nov 4, 2012

This morning is alright.

I hate when the food I'm eating doesn't have a wikipedia page.

It's cold out and my window is cracked open and I've got a sore little bump on the back of my neck.

It could be a pimple-in-the-making, like a celebrity.

The weather has been beautiful, if cold, everyday since the hurricane.

When nature imposes itself, needs a little attention, does something like destroy homes and people, it's hard not to forgive it after the first or second clear sky.

That's the sort of relationship I want.

Wait. No. That's bad. Sorry.

I should want a good relationship.

I should make it happen with Keila instead of just idly wanting it with some abstract person.

Keila's good after all. It's good when I'm with her I mean. I like being with her.

It's easy to forget that. It's easy to forget that when I only see her once every week or two.

I need to get a car.

God damn it.

Look. Look. Fuck. Look.

Okay. I'm okay.

Sometimes its better to stop typing then to have never typed at all.

I'll never get the *than vs. then* rule right the first time.

But there's something you should know about me.

I'm easily alienated and invitations make it worse.

Oh yeah and I'm intensely insecure.

Oh and I do this cool thing where I'm a total fucking asshole sometimes and I hate myself.

And I really appreciate aggressive hugs.

Oh and I don't know how to be in a relationship where I'm not immediately in love.

And when I am immediately in love, I don't know how to react when it settles.

Oh and I got this really cool thing going where if I don't think you're an asshole, I think I'm the asshole, because someone is always the asshole.

Oh, and before I forget, when I was nine I broke a first-grader's arm because, as I told the teacher, my power can't be contained.

And sometimes when I see a pretty girl, I look at her face and think, I want to be the person who ruins everything for you.

I want to be the reason why you feel bad.

Then I get to feel bad about it.

## Tuesday, November 6, 2012

This morning the lines are cut off.

There's no communicating with the outside world.

The weatherman told everyone to look the forecast up online before giving his two weeks notice.

My window has grown to a new thickness and all I can do is see through it.

Why don't I make more of an effort with Keila.

Why don't I try just a little bit harder.

That's all it takes. That's all anything takes. That little bit is all that matters.

I feel this tremendous thing that has the potential to make me cry but never does, and the potential, most of the time, is enough. But I envy people who cry, envy their definitive catharsis, how they feel something and their body reacts accordingly.

That's why I let my hands dry out in the winter.

As I begin to feel weighted things more heavily, insisting on being unprepared, appealing for a kind of emotional justice as I grow permanently older, I wonder if deciding to relent, and fully feel what's due, makes me any less who I was.

Is this the way to stay the same.

To rope off the emotional capacity of younger selves and say no more.

Consistency is valued in our society.

But if time is linear and everyday is new, remaining the same is impossible.

So each day there is this lottery, whether who I am will be less or more who I was, or who I want to be.

Most of the time, when we communicate with someone, we understand the words they are going to use before they use them. That's speaking the same language.

And if we all know the same words, give or take a few, then why bother exchanging them.

Trying to do anything is the hardest thing to do.

Nothing is out to hurt you.

You are out to be hurt.

## IDEAS II:

A tattoo of two people wanting to talk to each other in an elevator.

An indie rock band called *Sad and Male.*

An online dating site called *Emotionally unavailable but still needy.*

A 24-hour news network called *We just like money.*

A *criticism* section on animals' wikipedia pages.

A game show called *Who's having the least fun?*

An indie movie called *Here's some stuff about life you already understand.*

A new thing called *Basically the old thing.*

A prescription drug called *I used to be a kid.*

A bottled water company called *We really didn't think this would catch on.*

## Wednesday, November 7, 2012

It's the first snow of the year.

First came rain. Before the rain left, snow arrived.

They overlapped and fell down together long enough for it to feel emotional.

Snow, lighter than rain, falls slower.

Gradually, though, it overtook the rain and fell faster in victory.

Close to my window the snow fell to the right.

Farther from my window, maybe thirty feet forward, the snow fell to the left.

The branches got heavy.

Wind carries the snow in sweeping billows.

It would feel incredible to be pushed along by these billows, dressed warmly in winter coats a hundred feet long.

Last year it snowed so early, the trees still had all their leaves. The weight of the snow grew too much, and the trees fell down.

The snow hurt them then.

I see Keila friday.

# THINGS:

How is it a comfort that things can always be worse.

Why does this letter look like that: e

One time my brother's dog was eating butter so my grandma took a can of cream soda and poured it all over the dog. I asked her, "Why did you pour soda on the dog?" and she just laughed.

Sometimes when I sit on the subway and the person next to me slides down a couple seats I think about silently sliding down next to them again.

There is a language barrier in talking to people who have their shit together.

The best I've ever felt has been in passing moments too quick to hold on to.

Date me once, wake up to my passive-aggressive emails for life.

## Thursday, November 8, 2012

Today on my lunch break I sat down with a coffee on a park bench.

Two girls nervously sat down at the other end with their food.

One looked down at her meal and said, “They only gave me one falafel.”

The other replied, “That’s so gay, falafel.”

## Friday, November 11, 2012

I open my web browser.

I stare at a blank tab for several minutes then open a new one.

I remember spending 30 minutes walking around the neighborhood pretending to be a ghost. Only dogs were allowed to sense me. Everyone else I got mad at.

I never do that stuff anymore.

Part of getting older is getting depressed when things that used to make you happy only serve to remind you of the person you once were.

Now I just feel like a security camera for my emotions, watching them suspiciously from a corner.

I count the number of people that care about me. This is the minimum number of people I will hurt.

It's time to leave for the bus to see Keila.

# A NEW ABC SITCOM CALLED:

A new abc sitcom called *Unemployed* where the protagonist wakes up, checks tumblr, gets distracted by porn and idly masturbates for a while.

A new abc sitcom called *An unfunny portrayal of personal failure in a depressed economy.*

A new abc sitcom called *A young married couple that is too scared to get a divorce so they have a kid but that doesn't seem to help either.*

A new abc sitcom called *It's literally impossible to meet the expectations of your parents because they didn't know you when they decided to have you.*

## Tuesday, November 13, 2012

In life there is usually someone nearby having a really intense time doing a really boring thing.

Some people can have a really intense experience waiting in line at the post office.

They can be seething with hatred and murder, imagining the precise, agile incisions they would make along the femoral arteries of everyone counting out stamps and filling out international shipping forms.

Intensity isn't in action, but perception. You don't need to skydive to feel it.

And these people, who experience an intensity among the rest of us, are the protagonists of their own film.

They are constantly integrating events of their life into a dramatic narrative, including both highs and lows but never anything in between.

Getting broken up with or buying a food processor is just as important as getting a dream job or fancy sports car.

Everything becomes its own vital scene.

These people are usually ambitious. They usually view life as having some kind of ultimacy. Something to work toward, struggle for, live against.

And in this way, there's always something to talk about, there's always something to think about, there's always an immediacy to life, the illusion of a grasp on the world, dismay for what's been and excitement for what's to come. Happiness in it's way.

I must seem so tired in comparison.

## SLOGAN FOR INSECURITY:

*Something for everyone.*

## Wednesday, November 14, 2012

Keila and I are alive at the same time.

Many people have been alive before me and will be alive after me, but her and I occupy this same stretch right now.

I look at her, somewhere not quite her eyes, but the space before them.

I look at her and think about how all of us, right now, are living and breathing and talking.

We're all alive.

Most people are just better at it than we are.

## Thursday, November 15, 2012

The reality of the digital age, for me, is lying supine on the floor with a glowing rectangle, sometimes touching it, other times laughing at it or feeling sad because of it.

I get out of the shower and look in the mirror. I feel alone the way some people are left handed.

Keila says life is just a way to measure time.

She says she is good at hiding things and I think about feelings.

## Friday, November 16, 2012

The worst part of talking to people is when they want you to respond.

Most people have more efficient ways of dealing with their emotions than writing books.

My ideal editor would tell me she hates me and my book and she regrets publishing me and everyone else she's ever published and that she should've just gone to law school or gotten a business degree because fiction and poetry are dying and it's the fault of people like her.

My second most ideal editor is a blind feral three-legged corgi.

Dick like gogurt.

## Sunday, November 18, 2012

The world's loneliest cephalopod, Henry The Hexapus, is in captivity, studied for being the only octopus born with six tentacles.

I part with all things all the time. I turn off televisions like an athlete tears tendons.

I know what it's like, this life.

I've got experience.

I've felt sadness in all the places I've been.

I've seen Swiss Alps from above and ridden horses through Arizona deserts and hiked alone through Colorado's red mountains and all the while felt hostile, like I'm missing something beautiful, like there's a color to nature I'm blind to or a language embedded that I can't speak, that the world is a sculpture too modern for me to appreciate and too historic to feel nostalgia for.

And I've tried to remove constructs and fictions, I've tried to see like a child, I've tried but you can never remove yourself from your perception, and I'm looking for forgiveness.

And I know that everyone is capable of doing to me the injury of differences between people.

And I know that all pain leads to the same primal fear and insecurity that there's no fun at all, there's no relief, there's no decision to be made, there's only this, which has been given to you instead of everything you wish life was, and that behind it all is only a pitch darkness, emptier than the space we forget we float in.

So I feel you Henry.

## Tuesday, November 20, 2012

Upon waking this morning I remembered telling myself, *Don't forget to look up cat-people on wikipedia.*

I got up and drank tea instead of coffee. I gargled mouthwash instead of brushing.

I took a shower and watched a swatch of different pubic hairs swirl around and around, tracing small tornados above the drain, terrorizing microscopic cities.

I peeled tangerines over a plate of crumbs from the toast I ate a few days before.

I sat and tried to think nothing.

I put on a podcast I listened to in high school. Karl Pilkington talked about how he used to wake up at 5:30am to get ready for work in the morning when he had his old job.

It was those early hours that were always the worst for him, having to get showered, assemble his things, and leave for his commute to the office before the sun was up.

On vacation Karl didn't want to sleep through those early hours because then they would pass right by him unappreciated. So in his hotel he set his alarm for 5:30 so that he could wake up and enjoy not going anywhere.

I'm at the Crosby now, seated at the white picnic table, drinking coffee out of the behandled mason jar.

I become more attracted to the barista here each time. It almost means something, maybe about learning.

A guy in this cafe just sat down next to a woman and said, "Hey, what's your name?" and she replied "Jenna," and the guy said, "Nice to meet you Hannah" and I felt terrible.

I'm sitting by the window at the end of the picnic table. The windows, long and rectangular and three in a row, have a crawling frost rooted at the bottom near the sill.

I can't tell if I'm on the right side of it to draw with my fingers, and I'm afraid of finding out.

A quiet togetherness lingers in certain things after Keila goes back to her campus. Because she's in school full-time and I'm at work five or six days a week, we only see each other once in a while. I try to visit her when I can, but she has a car and a license.

She'll come over for a night and a morning, then one of us will leave after breakfast.

For the week after she leaves there's an even slower departure, as I smell her less and less on my towel that she borrowed after showering, or on my pillowcase that we shared while I slept so well in her hair.

It's as if we only go a few days apart if I pay close enough attention to these things. It's as if we're together longer.

Feeling the way I do having written that, I can tell it's all ending.

# RECOMMENDATIONS:

Being a part of as many unsatisfying relationships as possible.

Finding different ways to be alone.

Melted cheese.

Most dogs.

Organizing your life around things that probably won't work out.

Fucking up over and over but in new and interesting ways.

Sharing everything you can remember about yourself.

Viewing all emotions as equal.

Seeing everyone as an attempt.

Feeling confused by the phrase *Be yourself.*

Assuming everyone has been mistreated at various points in their life.

Letting it all hit you.

## Sunday, November 25, 2012

The ease of getting out of bed is what makes it so difficult.

My face feels stretched like a canvas over a frame.

A shitty canvas. A shitty frame.

I'm drinking coffee. I'm sitting at my desk. I'm facing the window.

It's almost—keep going—almost a nice day.

The sky is cloudy and it might snow or rain.

Between the clouds though you can see the blue behind.

It's there. The blue sky is there I just can't see it right now.

I take a breath and when I exhale I receive more thoughts.

I look down into my coffee and see the top of my window reflected back and it moves in an otherworldly way.

The dark watery reflection closes in on the sky and I see the blue appear.

I look up and see that it's gone.

I lower my gaze and know the difference between wanting to talk to people and talking to people.

I draw a portrait of myself standing when I'd rather be lying down.

I never get the nose right.

Then I find I have realized nothing, but still have a feeling of revelation. It's like a failed take-off where nothing went wrong but the plane is still on the ground, and everyone decides that's enough, and they head home with a sense of accomplishment.

I've been eating these frozen pancakes that I take out of the box and tear out of the plastic sleeve and place in the toaster.

They are frozen into pairs, two circular halves, like a pre-sliced hamburger bun, as if there's a seam loosely stitched between them.

I peel them apart like I'm trying to find something.

## Friday, December 7, 2013

I had a wisdom tooth pulled.

I've been taking more vicodin than I should.

I tried to end things with Keila yesterday.

She's really good at not getting broken up with, and I'm really good at being a lonely person.

I told her she is learning to be independent.

I'm waiting for the vicodin to kick in.

Keila …

I can see myself with her though, I can.

But I don't think that's enough, because these things always have a way of ending.

It's a kind of fatalism.

I'm not a believer in marriage, but if I know that I can't eventually feel happy years down the line looking back at the moment I'm currently in … If I can see an ending to the relationship, even if that ending is years down the line … then it comes so much sooner. It cuts off everything that would've come before it.

I see her again on Sunday.

## Sunday, December 9, 2012

Today is gray. There is no hope in the sky.

It's a punishing kind of gray, the kind we get when we deserve it.

The kind of gray that says, you've hurt people, you've let them down.

If I'm responsible for anything, it's all my actions always.

I used lazy clichés and Keila called me out on it.

I said, "You're learning to walk. If we continue you'll learn with a crutch.

She said, "You don't know what's going to happen."

I said, "I'm doing this because I have no choice."

She said, "You do have a choice."

She said, "You have two options and you're choosing the sad one."

## Thursday, December 27, 2012

I boil water for coffee but don't make any.

I think about eating but don't eat.

I think about writing but don't write.

I lie down and my thoughts sink into the pillow.

I go into old memories and give up inside them.

I move forward into more recent memories and do the same.

I return to the present where I am trying to alter the past.

I sit down in the present and look around and think blanks until it's all white, or a blue so airy that it's just emissions and skin-felt waves. I stare a mental gif of the ocean. I want to be in it, or over it, or beneath it, somewhere inside the code. I think about trains that might take me to the ocean and I wonder if they run in the winter.

I pause to think about the winter and it's a thought like a place.

I think about how many times I have the thought that I want to be a better person and think that the number is huge, so huge that it prevents me from thinking anything else.

Desire takes the place of action and I just sit with it.

I sit and reach for the computer.

I look at its battery.

I envy how often it dies.

## Friday, December 28, 2012

My chest is bruised from coughing.

My room is too warm. Situated on the second floor, it gets proximity heat from the apartments above and below. The proximity is a reminder.

Sitting at this desk, the cold outside and the heat in here, it's impossible to feel comfortable.

Feeling alienated by my capability to feel differently.

Imagining comfort as sitting beside someone in bed, leaned against the headboard, hands achieving smallness, drawing outlines or finishing something without reward, private things in the company of another, brains being brains rather than the parents of bodies, information coming in to be processed without hesitation, without forms to fill out or quick glances left and right, silence more than talking and not having a preference about what to do now or next, touching arms without moving thoughts into the skin, light warmth, lighter than clothes, feeling capable of this, and yet feeling none of it.

## Tuesday, January 1, 2013

There are always new years and old ones, and every year they just get newer and older.

My favorite emotion in 2012 was how I felt upon realizing it's much later in the day than I thought.

My favorite thing to say to people in 2012 was whatever they had just said to me, only more quietly.

My favorite tension in 2012 was the kind where you both sense what's about to happen next, as if the future can be understood twice.

## Monday, January 7, 2013

My friend has an old angry cat.

They were both little when she got her. They ate together, played together, slept together.

It started to change as they got older. My friend found herself less enamored with the kitten as it became a cat. She lost interest in waving a toy around when there were friends to call and essays to turn in.

She recalls the cat put up a bit of a fight at first, meowing loudly as she began to come home late, my friend too overwhelmed with the new pace of her adolescent life to entertain a pet.

The cat however, receiving less and less attention, began eating more instead. An ingenious new electric dispenser ensured no person was attached to the food that kept it alive through the years.

Now, over a decade later, my friend visiting her parents' over the holidays, exercising the careful understanding and patience that this new adult ritual requires, remembers her cat as they used to be. She asks her parents and they can't remember when they threw her favorite toy away.

## SELECTIONS FROM WIKIPEDIA'S LIST OF DOGS THAT REMAINED LOYAL AFTER THEIR OWNER'S DEATHS:

After Lao Pan, a poor 68-year-old Shandong villager who lived alone, died in November 2011, his home was cleared, and his unnamed yellow dog disappeared. Villagers later noticed the dog had found Lao Pan's grave. They tried to bring the dog back to the village, but the dog refused to leave the grave. They tried luring him with some with some buns, but he took the food and ran back to the site again. Villagers felt touched by the dog's behavior, arranged to provision him daily at the grave, and as of a week later when the first reports appeared, had decided to build him a shelter there.

In 1924, Hidesaburō Ueno, a professor in the agriculture department at the University of Tokyo, took in Hachikō, a golden brown Akita, as a pet. During his owner's life, Hachikō greeted him at the end of each day at the nearby Shibuya Station. The pair continued their daily routine until May 1925, when Professor Ueno did not return. The professor had suffered from a cerebral hemorrhage and died, never returning to the train station where Hachikō was waiting. Every day for the next nine years the dog waited at Shibuya station for his owner.

## Tuesday, January 8, 2013

I like boiling pasta because it's loud at first, the pots in the cupboard, then quiet after.

I like doing sad things because it is more productive than feeling sad things.

I hear sirens outside, through the crack in my window, and an ambulance honking.

Someone, somewhere, made a mistake today.

## Friday, January 18, 2013

I had a dream I was in love with someone but I can't remember who.

I feel the warmth of the sun through my window and wonder how long it will remain this pleasant.

How long does that take.

When do you start to want something else.

I take a sip of water and now I am going to open the window.

The answer is in moments.

When I think of Keila it's forced.

You can basically forget about her.

## Sunday, January 20, 2013

As I drink this coffee I begin to feel changes in the frontal part of my headface.

I feel pressure In my sinuses, in the tubes that justify my nose, the area behind my eyes, it's heavy.

I allow that physical pressure to replace my emotions.

My sinuses can carry that burden for a while.

In this economy, we all need to do our part.

## Monday, January 21, 2013

Being single I remember that I'm not good at it.

I never feel comfortable around strangers, I never do well in bars.

I don't charm easily, or come off how I want to. I've never had a one-night stand.

I'm really bad at small talk with people I'm attracted to.

I am good, however, at wearing a friendship down into a relationship, carving out my niche, leaving it empty and ruining both of us.

Just a different skillset.

You know?

## Tuesday, January 22, 2013

This morning I watched a porno with the premise that a poor couple needs money, so they find someone online who will pay to come have sex with the girl while her boyfriend watches.

The tension in the video, though manufactured, was still palpable as the boyfriend watched his girlfriend suck another guy off.

I masturbated to it, identifying more with the despondent boyfriend than with the person receiving the blowjob.

Now I'm here. Which used to seem like enough.

When I was younger I thought my existence in time and space was justification for what I felt I deserved.

I would sit in classrooms like I was fulfilling a crucial role, occupying this crucial desk, listening to these words that require my ears.

I would raise my hand like everyone was impressed with how I turned oxygen into carbon dioxide.

I would talk to my friends like the space I removed with my mass was brighter and more important.

I learned, though.

I'm a destructive thing on this earth, occupying a portion of time where the amount of living people outnumber the dead.

I walk around thinking that the police don't protect people from each other. Not really.

I walk around knowing that I am here to hurt people, that I hurt Keila, that I'm guilty, and no one is doing anything about it.

## Wednesday, January 23, 2013

I feel the sun again, though I'm at my brother's apartment.

Sometimes I sleep here, wake up to find him gone and his dog staring at me.

I grind the coffee beans he buys and put on the kettle he got for christmas a couple years ago.

I walk by his dog on my way from the kitchen to the bathroom and reach down to pet it.

The dog doesn't want to be pet because it's worried about my brother.

There's no way the dog can know where my brother went, where he is now, or when he'll be back.

The dog doesn't know how to use a cellphone.

I set up a table in front of my brother's window and roll the shade up to let the light in.

Fabricating circumstance to fabricate feelings.

Feelings are just thoughts that gave up.

Almost every human action can be explained by insecurity.

Every time I wake up and get out of bed I think I can turn everything around.

If I didn't think that I wouldn't get out of bed.

Every time I shower I think I can turn everything around.

If I didn't think that I wouldn't shower.

Some days, in terrible voices, I lay in bed well after the alarm goes off.

Putting on pants and walking out the door to the bodega in flip-flops despite the January cold is the emotion that belongs to *time goes forward with or without me*.

I want to sing a chorus of words so helpless they sound like feelings.

I want to sing that chorus while sitting in the chair my father wore his shape into.

Wherever I am, I am always leaving.

The average amount of time it takes to complete this process is 78.2 years.

Will someone tap me on the shoulder.

I wish you could see me illuminated by this window light.

I could recognize your cough from another room.

## Monday, January 28, 2013

It's been a while since discomfort was a motivating thing.

I don't know how many days old the coffee in this mug is.

I put my laundry in the washer on Friday and I still haven't moved it to the dryer.

Someone probably moved my wet clothes out of the machine and onto the floor so that they could wash their laundry too.

In the shower, for a few seconds, it felt as if someone were hugging me, playfully—how I imagine a young sister hugs her little brother. An act that feels how it was intended to.

I've never had a sister.

I never swim in pools because I'm afraid of bodies. I know how to dance but if you ask me I'll say I don't. The only way I know how to dance is secret and loving. I'm nine mistakes when you meet me.

## Monday, February 18th, 2013

There's a purposelessness to most actions, and yet we're wholly responsible for each and every one we make.

Humans are mostly on autopilot. Our brains are Plan B.

There's a beautiful disaster coming for all of us.

It will be bright like the morning and terrible like hanging up without saying bye.

Humor is the most malignant coping mechanism because it obscures what we should really consider by processing feelings into sound.

What if instead of laughing at irony, we got scared.

What if that fear made everything more fragile.

What if we were nice to each other again.

What if I reached over and pulled you close.

Would you shirk away.

Would you laugh?

## Tuesday, February 26, 2013

I'm seeing someone new.

She likes people who don't like themselves.

I like how many questions I get to ask her.

## Monday, March 4, 2013

Sometimes I send her texts and the texts have words but what they represent is something else.

Sometimes they represent *I like you.*

Other times, *Do you like me.*

Sometimes they ask questions like Have you heard of this band?

But they're trying to ask *Can you see us together for a long time?*

That same fatalism from before, knowing that one or both of us will feel very hurt because of the relationship we are trying to build, now feels different.

In the right light (this morning glows) that fatalism makes it all feel more intimate.

I am going to be the one to hurt you. You are going to be the one to hurt me. We are going to do this to each other and no one else right now. We're going to cause each other pain. I know this, okay. I won't hurt anybody else. Just you. I'll only hurt you and you'll only hurt me. We're in this together. We'll hurt each other together.

When she sleeps her breathing is so loud.

The volume of someone really trying.

## Wednesday, March 6, 2013

This new person I'm with, she could go on for days listing the different things she likes.

She could go on for weeks more about what she likes about those things.

It's a different way of seeing the world.

It's the kind of company that changes the tint of things. A replacement of lens. You want to keep seeing the world their way so you keep seeing them.

She comes over on weekends.

We watch movies but don't finish them.

We cut up fruit and eat it from the same bowl.

We listen to The Fray, or she lets me put on The Fray.

The beginnings of these things are like that.

The fucking best.

She goes to parties without me because I don't like parties and she texts me "This party isn't good, I should have stayed home with you."

She called my apartment home so quickly.

## Friday, March 8, 2013

I told her *I'm sorry I'm the thing you like.*

She touched my ears and poured me coffee.

We walked over to my bed and sat on it.

She told me I have a lot of beauty marks.

Calling them birthmarks is more appropriate because they are permanent and blameless.

She said, "There are so many on your arms."

This morning is the last snow of the season.

Saturday is going to be sunny and almost sixty degrees.

She and I made a lot of plans.

They include: walking outside, buying a plant, going to Ikea, going to the Prospect Park with my brother's dog, cutting my hair, baking a pie, listening to Slowdive and watching a movie.

But it happens in every friendship, and in relationships it's even worse, that first moment where you feel it, that there's no curiosity anymore, no feelings to share or things to do, and the park bench beneath your bodies becomes especially hard, and one of you looks at the other with eyes that are all apologies.

It's never like how you thought it would be for as long as you thought it would.

Everyday, satisfied or not, is comprised of opportunities lost.

My forehead, marked permanently by attempts at conveying sincerity. The way that, as a kid, I learned more complex and vulnerable ways of describing how I felt, while coming to understand that quicker and simpler descriptions are considered more polite, that these descriptions of things, real or not, don't lead me anywhere, like the vaguest of allegories, how one thing can be compared to the identification of the thing itself, how so much that matters ceases to upon any graduation, like deepening into oneself, falling asleep at night and not being able to remember what you did that day, how getting older transforms from accomplishment to regret, how memories depreciate like real estate.

But you can write a whole book.

You can call it anything you want.

You can print it out and stare at it.

On TV you swear you heard the President say that headaches are the growing pains of our emotions.

But by the time you read this I will be someone older and newer.

I will be ultimate. I will be somewhere else.

Blending with TV-colored walls.

Things can only get worse.

A loving kind of silence.

You, having left, then returned.

Me, having stayed, then stayed.

Mathematics and old movies.

The deaths of centuries inside you.

A hug that only comes apart.

A book you want to pull together.

A story that dies in your hands.

Apologies and thanks.

It'll be a new year again soon.

Spencer Madsen runs Sorry House. He tweets *@spencermadsen*.